Polka Dot
Rain Boots

By RL Lane

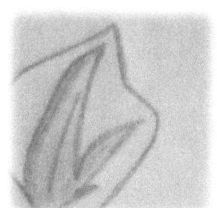

Illustrations and Photo Cover by RL Lane

"My feet pounded down on the pavement as I ran down the hill. I could barely see the orange and pink polka dots in the early morning light. They were good boots. They kept my feet mostly dry." RL Lane

He loved polka music…

It originated in Europe in the 1830s and made its way to America when people came from Eastern Europe. It is a fast style in 2/4 time, and often associated with the pre-World War II era. Polka still remains in America today. My Dad. He loved the polka music…

Well really he loved a lot of music. Oh…

You can't love a song if you don't have a soul

You can't feel the beat if you don't move your feet

'Round and 'round we go

Spinning through the air

Take away the sad as the sound floats through the air

Lift me up and put me down

Don't let me fall

Hold my hand and hug me tight

As the slow dance comes on

I'll close my eyes and think of you

I don't need to see you with my eyes

My heart can see you bright…

I know he looks down on me and tells me to keep that music playing…

But yet my house is so silent. Not a single sound from a television can be heard in the rooms. I can't drown the silence yet. I worked too hard to get the peace. Let me hear the peace. For just a while…

These stories are like my illustrations. I never know what these stories are about until I get to the end. I never know what I am drawing until I am done. How do I know when I am done? I just know…

I called this picture "step up and look around". I loved him from the start...

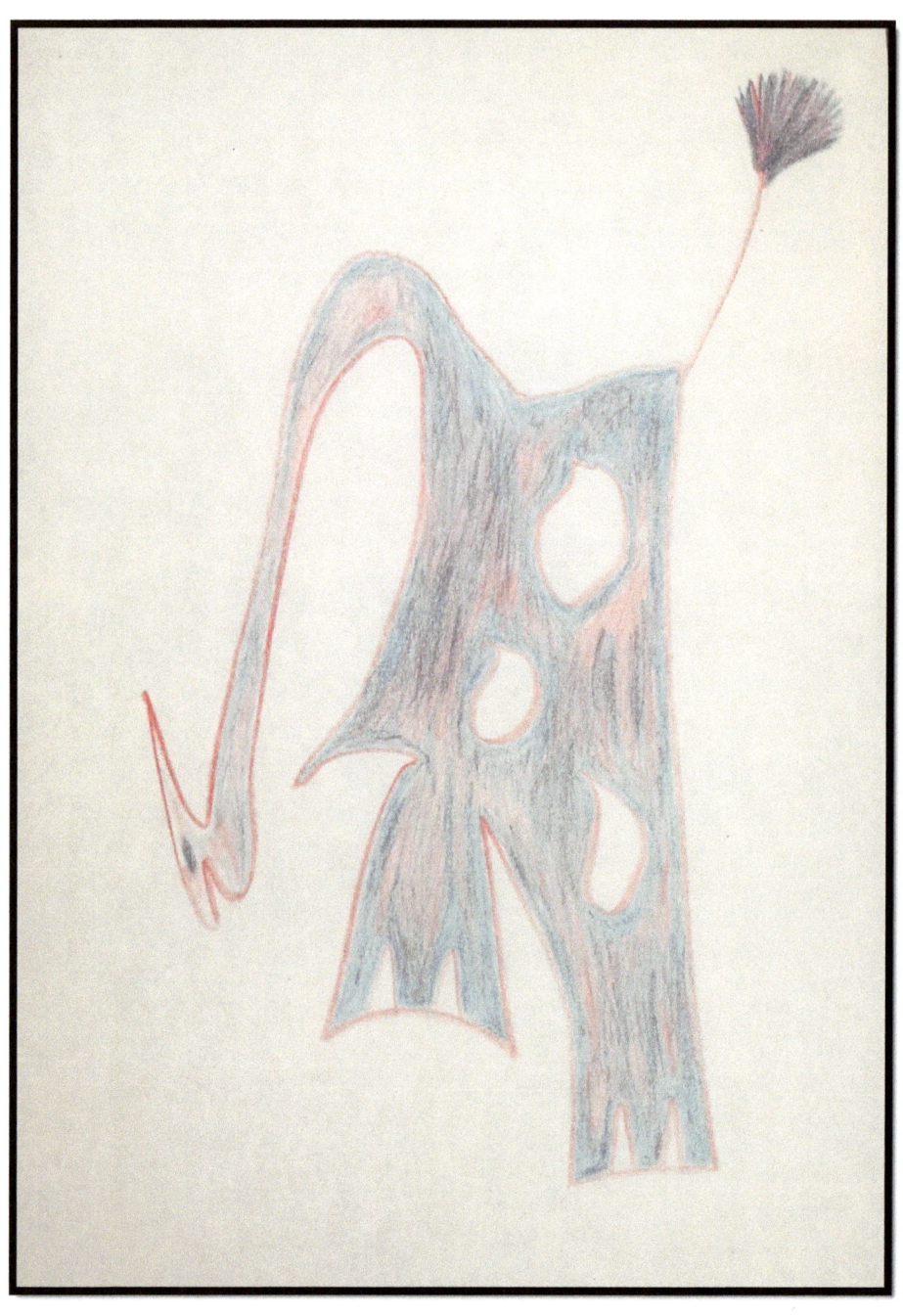

Especially because he is red, white and blue and his body pattern is like a tree trunk. My Dad loved our flag and he loved trees…

I see a hawk and its wing in the body. The neck is a swan…a symbol of love…

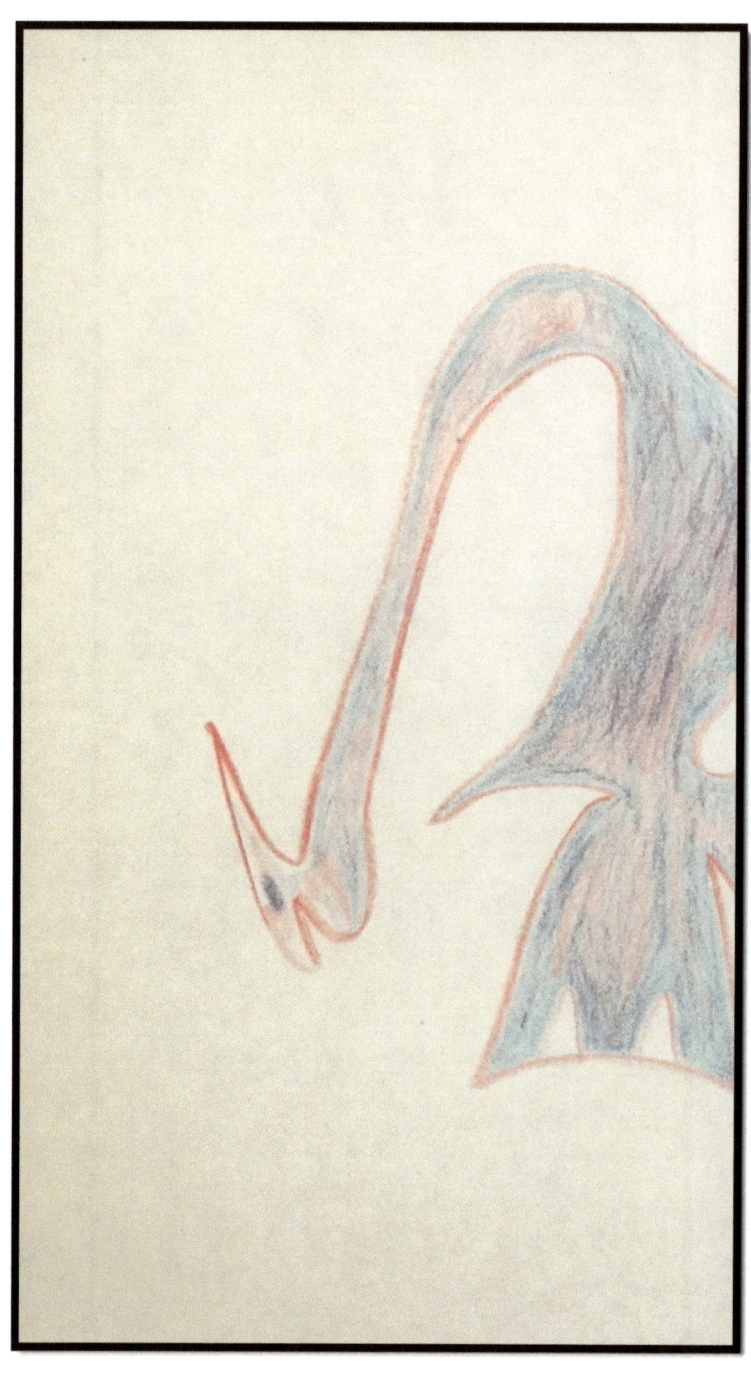

It has giant elephant feet. My Dad did not love elephants as far as I know. An elephant is forgetful, so they say…

My Dad would have reminded me to step up...and look around...really look around...all the way around...

What am I supposed to see Dad?

Do the nursing homes have music? I hope they all do. I hope I'll be able to hear the music until I leave the rock…

Why do I write so much about leaving this earth? Why can't I just write about the here and now? Who wants to be reminded our time here has a limit? Why can't I just love a day for every minute of its hours?

I don't even think I am afraid to go to the beyond. I am annoyed however that my body has to stay because I like what it can do…

Those polka dotted rain boots. I've had them for years. I didn't use them for the last few years. They were in my shed and I didn't want to get them out. It would have been so easy but I couldn't bring myself to do it. I have them out now again so my feet can be dry in the rain. Maybe I didn't care enough before to make sure they were protected. When you have too much going on in your life, you sometimes can't do the simplest of things…

I try to remember that when dealing with other people. I try to remember that humans like to hide their demons…

So I look for the polka dot rain boots…are people wearing them on the rainy days? It is not uncommon for others to struggle at points. Deaths and job losses and family fights and whatever other hurt comes along our way. Now I just say…

There must be a reason why they did not put on those…

Polka Dot Rain Boots.

About the Author and Illustrator

RL Lane has published the EcarreT series and a collection of short stories featuring the illustrations, along with the children's books "G" and "How to Catch a Goast". The series begins with "Chapel Street Signs"…

...unexplained connections that challenge us to beli ve. A woman, a Dad a Doctor, a cat and mouse, a horse and tale tell their stories. "Do you beli ve in spirits?" I asked my friend. "Well look", he said, "I believe there are things that cannot be explained..." Oh. Plus, hear ov a Mom's battle with her struggle to connect to the woman...her little girl.

Welcome to EcarreT...a world
Where everyone cares
Why did I have to create it in...

A fiction fantasy world?

You may already know why, but you will see regardless of what you believe as a girl's journey of love and faith on her "Touring Machine" take her on the best journey of her mundane life. A life well on its way takes a turn in a direction that could've never been seen or even dreamed...

The author can be contacted at:

RosaLeeeLane@gmail.com
www.Amazon.com/author/readrllane

Twitter.com/readrllane

Books by RL Lane

Chapel Street Signs

secret Life OV an antE

Sri Town

Which of EcarreT

Hand of Heven

Short Stories:

Mon Treal, The Odd Cod, The Half Day, No Gift for Greed, Aunt Elm & Uncle Poc, What Would Caitlin Wear, The Bag of Scribbles, Mr. Uraly's Italy, A not G, Johnni and Georg, A Cup of Butter, The Walk of a THOUSAND Moods, Storm Window, The Rugs, Cones of Ice Crème, Angel-A, The Art of Sri Town, Under Water, The Dinner Party, The Vault, No Lines to Erase, Rock of Snow

Children's:

G

How to Catch a Goast

www.ingramcontent.com/pod-product-compliance
Lightning Source LLC
Chambersburg PA
CBHW050912180526
45159CB00007B/2884